Floppy had not been for a walk.

"We should take Floppy out," said Mum.

Chip groaned, "Walking Floppy is boring."

"Well, you could bring the boomerangs," said Mum.

Biff threw her boomerang really hard. It flew up into the sky.

"I'll show them I'm not boring!" thought Floppy. "I'll make them laugh."

Floppy chased after the boomerang. Suddenly it turned in the air. Floppy turned as well.

"Mind the pond!" shouted Mum.

"Too late!" laughed Chip.

Splash! Floppy landed in the pond.

"Oh Floppy, you're filthy!" said Mum.

Everyone laughed. Floppy was pleased.

"At least I made them laugh," he thought.

Floppy was not so pleased when he got home. Mum wanted to give him a wash.

"Let's use the hose-pipe," she said.

"Oh no!" thought Floppy.

Floppy hid under Biff's bed.

"Why do I need a wash?" he thought. "Dogs like being dirty."

Suddenly, the magic key began to glow.

It was time for a new adventure.

"Dogs don't have magic adventures by themselves, do they?" thought Floppy. "Well, it's better than a bath."

The magic key took Floppy to Australia. It took him to a red desert. The sand was hot. It hurt Floppy's paws.

Suddenly, a boomerang flew over his head. Whoosh! Another one landed next to him. Then Floppy saw some men.

"Go away you dirty dingo!" they shouted.

Floppy ran away. The men chased him.
He ran past some rocks.

"Quick!" said a voice. "Hide here!"

The men ran past.

Behind the rocks were four dogs. They all laughed at Floppy.

"What floppy ears!" said one of them.

"What's your name?" asked another.

"Floppy," said Floppy.

"My name is Red," said Red. "This is Ginger, she's Amber, and he's called Tan. We're dingos."

"What's a dingo?" asked Floppy.

"That's what men call us," said Amber.

“Why did they chase me?” asked Floppy.

The dingos looked sad.

“We used to be friends,” said Tan. “But now men don’t like us because we have fleas.”

“We’ll show you,” said Red.

The dingos took Floppy to a cave. On the walls of the cave were paintings.

Some of the paintings were of animals Floppy had never seen before.

"These are very old paintings," said Amber. "They show a time when men and dingos lived together."

"We used to help men get food and sleep near their fires," said Red.

"If only we didn't have fleas," said Tan.

Outside the cave it was getting dark. The night was cold. Far away, the men had lit a fire.

"Let's hide near the men," said Red.

One of the men was telling a story. It was about a time long ago, when the world began.

"Those times long ago were called The Dreamtime," whispered Amber.

The story was about a creature called a kangaroo. The kangaroo wanted to steal fire from men.

Floppy was tired. He closed his eyes. He began to dream.

In Floppy's dream he met a strange animal with a long tail. It looked like one of the cave paintings.

"What's your name?" asked Floppy.

"They call me Kangaroo," he said.

Kangaroo wanted to make a fire. He rubbed two sticks together.

"This is how men make fire," he said.

Suddenly, the sticks caught fire. It made Kangaroo jump. He dropped the sticks.

The dry grass caught fire. The fire spread quickly. Kangaroo jumped up and down.

"It's hot! It's hot!" he said.

"Run to the water-hole," said Floppy.

All the animals ran to the water-hole. As they went into the water, fleas began to jump off their backs.

"Ah! Fleas don't like getting wet!" thought Floppy.

Floppy woke up. He had an idea.
He crept up to one of the men and picked up his boomerang.

"I have a plan," Floppy said to the dingos. "I think I can get rid of your fleas.

"You can?" said Amber. "Then we can make friends with the men."

"We need to find a water-hole," said Floppy.

"Follow us," said Red.

They walked for a long time. At last, they got to the water-hole.

“Pick up the boomerang,” said Floppy. “And walk backwards into the water.”

Ginger walked backwards into the water. The fleas on his legs began to crawl on to his back. They did not want to get wet.

"Keep going!" said Floppy.

Ginger went deeper. Soon his back was under the water. The fleas crawled on to his head. They did not want to get wet.

All the fleas were now on Ginger's head.

"Now put your head under the water," said Floppy.

Ginger lay down in the water. The fleas crawled up his nose and on to the boomerang.

“Let go of the boomerang!” said Floppy. The boomerang floated away. The fleas stayed on the boomerang.

“Hooray!” cheered the dingos.

“Now we can all get rid of our fleas and make friends with the men,” said Amber.

“I hope so,” said Floppy.

The magic key began to glow. It was time for Floppy to go home.

"Oh no!" said Floppy. "I didn't bring anything back from my adventure."

Floppy heard Mum calling. She was still in the garden.

"Floppy! It's bath-time," she said.

Mum washed Floppy with the hose-pipe.
"Fleas!" she said. "How did you get fleas?"
Floppy picked up the boomerang.
"I'm off to the park," he thought. "I need to find a water-hole!"